~ VOLUME I ~

MAD ABOUT MARRIAGE

FLIPPING THE SWITCH
from "Just Plain Mad" to "Madly in Love" Forever!

PARTICIPANT GUIDE

LEGAL DISCLAIMER

Important: Unless the person who is facilitating this Mad About Marriage small group curriculum is a licensed counselor or psychologist, he or she is prohibited from giving marriage advice or offering marriage counseling. This Mad About Marriage small group curriculum is a marriage education product and is not to be considered or be a form of marriage counseling. The facilitator, unless he or she is a licensed counselor or psychologist, is legally and ethically prohibited from engaging in any form of marriage counseling and from dispensing marriage advice.

Books by Mike Tucker

Ten Keys to a Happy Marriage

Mad About Marriage

Mantras for Marriage

Every Good Thing

Jesus, He's All You'll Ever Need

Meeting Jesus in the Book of Revelation

Journal of a Lonely God

Jesus, Your Heart's Desire

A Time For You

Heart Food

Laws of Dating

~ VOLUME I ~

MAD
ABOUT MARRIAGE

FLIPPING THE SWITCH
from "Just Plain Mad" to "Madly in Love" Forever!

PARTICIPANT GUIDE | SIX SESSIONS

MIKE & GAYLE TUCKER

Mad About Marriage:

Flipping the Switch from "Just Plain Mad" to "Madly In Love" Forever!

Copyright ©2014 by Mike & Gayle Tucker

Requests for information should be addressed to:
curriculum@MadAboutMarriage.com

ISBN-10: 0991251814
ISBN-13: 978-0-9912518-1-0

Any telephone numbers, books, courses, Internet addresses, websites, blogs, social media channels, or other online properties printed in this book are offered as a resource. They are not intended in any way to be or imply an endorsement by Mad About Marriage, Faith For Today, or Mike & Gayle Tucker, nor does Mad About Marriage, Faith For Today, or Mike & Gayle Tucker vouch for the content of these sites and numbers for the life of this book.

All rights reserved. No part of this publication may be reproduced, stored in a retrieval system, or transmitted in any form or by any means – electronic, mechanical, photocopy, recording, or any other – except for brief quotations in printed reviews, without the prior permission of Mike & Gayle Tucker.

Design & Layout: Carter Design, Inc., Denver, Colorado

Printed in the United States of America

MadAboutMarriage.com

CONTENTS

INTRODUCTION — 1

SESSION 1 — 5
Good News: Your Marriage is Good Enough to Save

SESSION 2 — 21
Love & Respect: Avoiding the Marital Death Spiral

SESSION 3 — 37
Forgiveness: Healing Love's Deepest Wounds

SESSION 4 — 49
Marriage Myths: Damaging Myths About Relationships

SESSION 5 — 63
Intimacy & Desire: Getting That Loving Feeling Back!

SESSION 6 — 79
Commitment: Living Happily Ever After

"Happily ever after is not a fairy tale. It's a choice."

Fawn Weaver

INTRODUCTION

Taking Your Marriage Back To Happily Ever After

What is your attitude toward your marriage today?

Has it changed since that joyful day when you stood before the altar pledging to love your husband or wife for the rest of your life?

Has marriage become everything you hoped it would be and more? And are you as happy as you hoped you would be with the person of your dreams – that person who, at one time, you could not bear the thought of living without?

Is marriage more like a ball-and-chain or an exciting adventure?

For some, marriage is about restriction and loss of personal independence. But to others, it's about freedom and experiencing new realms of happiness, joy, and pleasure.

It's all about attitude.

Becoming "one flesh" with your wife or husband creates a new reality where it's possible to experience life on a higher and more wonderful level. Marriage unlocks a whole new dimension of happiness, and it can transform our lives from ordinary to extraordinary.

In a healthy marriage, we find the freedom and safety to be who we really are without fear of censure, ridicule, or rejection. Marriage is supposed to be a loving environment of trust, belonging, and hope.

Marriage: Happiness & Health

Research suggests that happily married people are healthier, have stronger immune systems, and live longer. The emotional support that marriage provides makes it easier to cope with life's pressures and stress. And knowing someone loves you inspires you to take better care of yourself, too. Besides, it's just nice to have someone to come home to at the end of the day, isn't it?

For Better or For Worse…

When you got married, you made a vow to stand by your mate no matter what, for better or worse, and your spouse took the same vow.

Imagine… having another human being in your life – your spouse – who will love and support you no matter what.

How does it feel to know that no matter how bad it gets, your husband or wife will never abandon you?

When times get tough, you have someone in your life you can count on. That thought alone fills the heart with peace and calm and reassures the spirit.

When we marry, we move from "me" to "we" – from "I" to "us." We start building a new life on the rock solid values of faithfulness, love, honesty, kindness, selflessness, charity, and respect.

Just Plain Mad or Madly In Love?

Happily married people realize marriage takes hard work. Failure to do the work may result in a life of frustration, conflict, and anger. Some husbands and wives become so angry with each other that they develop a negative attitude toward marriage in general. But does it really have to be this way?

We come back to the idea that marriage takes hard work. Human effort is the required investment to make marriage work so that love has a place to call home – our heart.

But there's more.

The Bible says in Genesis that God created love. In fact, He created marriage. There is a spiritual component to marriage – a divine element, if you will – which means that divine power is available to help you take your marriage from where it is right now to where you want it to be.

We don't know you or your story, but regardless of where you are right now, God has a plan for making your marriage better than you ever dreamed it could be. We encourage you to grasp the hand of the Divine as we take this "Mad About Marriage" journey.

If other couples have done it, so can you. We have seen countless husbands and wives experience God's power in a very personal way to turn struggling marriages into love-filled relationships and to grow good marriages into great ones.

So, where do we begin? Let's start with this core concept: Your marriage is good enough to save! You and your spouse have what it takes to be happy. You've woven a rich history, and each day, you are making memories that are stitching together your future. The power is yours to determine how beautiful that future will be.

~ Session 1 ~

Good News

Your Marriage is Good Enough to Save

"A successful marriage requires falling in love many times, always with the same person."

— Mignon McLaughlin

What You Will Discover in Session One

In session one, you will meet Willie and Elaine Oliver, authors of a hope-filled book titled: *Marriage in God's Hands*. Willie and Elaine inspire husbands and wives all over the world with the truth that their marriage is good enough to save, which is what they will talk about in this session.

Opening Prayer

God specializes in putting broken pieces back together and restoring marriages. So let's invite His presence into our group and dedicate this hour to Him as we discover that our marriages are good enough to save.

"Father God, we thank You for Your grace and loving compassion. We are so grateful for Your power and forgiveness. And we look forward to our time together with You and each other as we discover how to have a healthy and happy marriage. Please help us to be madly in love. In Your name we pray. Amen."

CONNECTING QUESTION

Before our group watches the video of Willie and Elaine, let's check to see how we feel about the radical idea that our marriages are good enough to save.

Question: What do you think a "good enough" marriage is – and how do you know if you have one?

SESSION ONE NOTES:

Willie & Elaine Oliver with Mike & Gayle Tucker

_____
_____
_____
_____
_____
_____
_____
_____
_____
_____
_____
_____

> *"I've been asked, 'How do I know if I'm married to the right person?' It's nice to have a simple answer sometimes: If you're married, that's the right person. It's your duty to make that marriage the best it can be."*
>
> **David Jeremiah**
> Love, Marriage & Sex: The Song of Solomon

EXECUTIVE SUMMARY

Good News: Your Marriage Is Good Enough to Save

Gaining a healthy and happy marriage requires a certain kind of attitude during the low points of your relationship, and it is this:

My Marriage is Good Enough to Save.

The Good News/Bad News About Low Points

According to researcher Dr. Paul R. Amato, most marriages that end in divorce in the United States are good enough to survive.

Think about that revelation for a moment. Imagine all of the husbands and wives who call it quits and lose their families because they feel that the pain of staying together hurts more than the pain of ending their relationship.

What causes them to lose hope? What pushes them over the edge of the marital cliff into divorce?

Tough times. Low points. Couples make the decision to end their marriage during the low points of their relationship. But if they decided to stay together during the low points, then guess what? They would have high points again!

The bad news about low points is that they are a part of life and cause far too many couples to call it quits. But the good news is that low points don't last – they are not permanent!

A Word About Feelings

Feelings are fleeting; they come and go. Many people are getting divorced based on how they FEEL today. Feelings follow behavior. Today, you might not feel as much love for your spouse or feel loved by them, but if you do loving things, then loving feelings will return.

If you are going through a low point in your marriage, please hang on and don't give up. You are struggling through a temporary situation that can be repaired. To choose to end your marriage right now would be like someone choosing to amputate a broken arm instead of letting the bone heal.

Wouldn't you agree that it is unwise to use a permanent solution to "fix" a temporary problem?

If you are frustrated and hurting because your relationship is struggling through a low point right now, then be encouraged because things will get better. Your high point is on the way. You will be happy again.

The Truth About Divorce

According to research, people who get divorced are no happier three years later. And, additionally, children from divorced families don't do as well in school or eat as well. In fact, depending on their age at the time of divorce, they may deal with separation anxiety, abandonment issues, and other psychological and emotional challenges.

Choosing to stay together for the well-being of the children is great motivation to go the extra mile in working things out. Couples that decide to stay together for the sake of the kids and do whatever it takes to restore their marriage admit it is one of the best decisions they ever made and are so glad they did.

Dynamic Versus Static Factors

Dr. Scott Stanley, University of Denver, talks about dynamic factors versus static factors. Most people get divorced over what he calls dynamic factors – factors that can be changed.

Static factors are things that cannot be changed easily or at all, such as your parents having been divorced; you can't change it, and it's something that could affect your marriage.

But these are a few dynamic factors you can change:

§ Your attitude

§ How you communicate with each other

§ How you resolve conflict

§ Dysfunctional attitudes

§ Disempowering beliefs

What is your attitude about your marriage? In your heart, do you believe it is good enough to save and that you and your spouse can be happy again? If so, then you can work through any challenge you may be facing now or in the future.

Is Your Marriage Good Enough?

What is a "good enough" marriage, and how do you know if you have one?

Let's keep this real simple. A good enough marriage isn't a perfect marriage, because no marriage is perfect. A good enough marriage will have its share of high points and low points; welcome to life.

A good enough marriage is one in which most of the conflicts revolve around dynamic factors – things that can be changed – versus static factors; things that cannot be changed.

Your Outlook Determines Your Outcome

Your outlook regarding your spouse and marriage determines whether you will go the distance or call it quits.

What is your outlook? Do you wake up feeling: "I'm stuck in this lousy marriage!"?

Or, do you wake up choosing to think and feel: "My marriage is good enough to save, and I'm committed to doing whatever it takes to have an outstanding relationship with this wonderful person that I'm so blessed to have in my life."

A Convenient Truth

Here is the most important truth that we want you to grasp from today's session. Cling to it with all of your heart, mind, and soul:

The person you fell in love with is STILL in your marriage with you today.

Do what it takes to have a happy marriage that endures.

Invest the energy and effort to have a healthy relationship.

Put your marriage in God's hands so that your love lasts forever.

Remember the story from the video of the unfaithful husband and his wife who chose forgiveness even though she wanted to call it quits? One of her favorite things is hearing her daughter say, "Daddy's home!" She knew in her heart she had made the right decision when she watched her husband help their little girl put the star on the top of their Christmas tree. Her heart beamed with joy as her husband looked back at her and mouthed the words, "Thank you." It was a moment that never would have happened without forgiveness.

Their marriage was worth saving, and so is yours.

You and your spouse deserve a marriage that overflows with happiness, playfulness, and love for the rest of your lives.

You will never regret saving your marriage and staying together.

GROUP DISCUSSION

1. After hearing and watching the video of Willie and Elaine, what is your response to their claim that most marriages are good enough to save?

2. According to Dr. Scott Stanley, marriages may have dynamic factors and/or static factors. What is the difference between dynamic and static factors?

3. For most marriages that end in divorce, was it dynamic or static factors that ended the relationship?

4. What impact, if any, should children have on whether a husband and wife should divorce?

5. As people of faith, we don't have to save, or grow, a marriage on our own. We're not saying marriage isn't difficult. But what role do you think God fills in having a happy and healthy marriage?

6. Willie and Elaine state that a healthy, happy marriage is possible, but only if you DECIDE it's possible. In your own thoughts and words, what do you think they mean?

7. Willie and Elaine suggest that doing loving things encourages loving feelings to return. Has this principle ever been true in your experience, or have you ever seen it in action?

ASSIGNMENT ONE: CONNECTING WITH YOURSELF

Self-Reflection Questions

1. A "good enough" marriage is one in which most of the conflicts revolve around dynamic factors (things that can be changed) versus static factors (things that cannot be changed).

2. What do you think? Do you have a marriage that is good enough to save?

3. Evaluate any relational conflicts that may exist between you and your spouse. Would you say that they are more static or dynamic in nature?

4. How do you feel about divorce: Is it true that divorce is a permanent solution to a temporary problem? What did you think about the illustration that was used in the Executive Summary, that deciding to get divorced is like choosing to amputate an arm instead of giving the bone time to heal? To what degree is this true or not true?

5. Are you willing to invest your highest and best energies to do whatever it takes to save your marriage, or to make it even better if you already have a happy marital relationship?

6. What do you think it would take from you to have the marriage of your dreams?

ASSIGNMENT TWO: CONNECTING WITH YOUR SPOUSE

INSTRUCTIONS: Do this exercise first by yourself, and then share and discuss your answers with your spouse:

PART I: List five reasons why you married your spouse. In the beginning, what did you love so much about this person that you wanted to spend the rest of your life together?

1.

2.

3.

4.

5.

ASSIGNMENT TWO: CONNECTING WITH YOUR SPOUSE

Part II: When you change your thoughts, habits, and attitudes, you change your mind and create a different result. When a husband and wife make these changes, their marriage can go from being good enough to GREAT!

Affirm and encourage each other right now by acknowledging this truth:

"We can do this AND we WANT to do this!"

Now, together, answer and discuss this question:

"What can we do to make our marriage better?"

Really pour yourselves into this process and take the time you need to answer these questions. If you don't get through them all right now, decide on a time in the coming days to meet and complete this process:

1. What attitudes do we need to change in order to have a healthier and happier marriage?

2. What habits do we need to change to have a healthier and happier marriage?

3. What beliefs do we need to change about each other, or about the dynamic/static factors in our relationship, in order to have a healthier and happier marriage?

Commitment: Commit to stay together no matter what. Do whatever you need to do to be happy together and have a healthy marriage. Decide right now that, no matter what, you will stay together and join forces to improve your marriage.

CATALYST

Based on what we've learned in session one, here are some reminders, questions, or action steps to move you from where you are to where you want to be – from a good marriage to a great one. Choose one or two that you will do this week before session two:

1. Decide to change your attitude. What will your new attitude be?

2. Start doing the things that you did when you were dating.

3. Play together. Get out and play games, go shopping, do stuff together. Schedule a date night for this week to reconnect with your spouse.

4. Compliment your spouse. "I like the way you walk." "I like the way you smile." "I like the way you _____."

5. Write your story: Play the "Fifty Years From Now" game from the video: What will we want to remember and cherish 50 years from now? What will we have lost?

6. Solve your solvable problems. Dr. John Gottman says some problems can't be solved, but focus on the ones that can. You will need to compromise because when you're married, you're no longer an "I"; you are an "US."

7. Change your thinking. Say, "I'm in a good enough marriage. Now, what do I need to do to make this marriage better?" Example: Gardening. It requires a lot of time and dedication – the right soil, right lighting, etc. If we can do that for our flowers, then we can do that for our marriage. Take the attitude of "I'm trapped" and turn it into the attitude of "I get to spend another day with this man or this woman who is so awesome, a person who I wanted and chose to spend the rest of my life with!"

(continued on next page)

8. Evaluate your hearing: Are you listening to understand each other or just passing each other by? Decide to listen AND understand each other. Otherwise, you will grow apart and feel alienated.

9. Remind yourself of this relationship truth daily: If we're not intentionally growing together, we are intentionally growing apart.

10. Spend time together. Make "together time" a priority. Invest time in what is most important. When you do this, your marriage will thrive, stabilize, and go from good to great!

RESOURCES

- *Marriage in God's Hands*, Willie and Elaine Oliver
- *Good Enough Marriages*, Dr. Paul R. Amato
- *Dynamic Factors Versus Static Factors*, Dr. Scott Stanley, University of Denver
- *The Seven Principles For Making Marriage Work*, Dr. John Gottman, Seattle Marital and Family Institute

NEXT WEEK, SESSION TWO

Love & Respect: Avoiding the Marital Death Spiral

Virtually all problems in marriage boil down to a lack of love and respect. In Session Two, we will learn why this happens and how to turn it around.

~ SESSION 2 ~

LOVE & RESPECT

AVOIDING THE MARITAL DEATH SPIRAL

"Every good relationship, especially marriage, is based on respect. If it's not based on respect, nothing that appears to be good will last very long."

~ AMY GRANT ~

LOVE & RESPECT

What You Will Discover in Session Two

In session two, you will meet Dr. Emerson Eggerichs, author of *Love & Respect,* and the Founder and President of Love and Respect Ministries. According to his research, love best motivates a woman, and respect most powerfully motivates a man. His ministry works with thousands of couples worldwide to help them restore their marriages.

Opening Prayer

The Bible says that God is love. He created marriage and performed the first wedding. So, if there is anyone from whom we can learn how to love more deeply, it is God. The Bible has much to say, too, about respect; It encourages wives to respect their husbands and husbands to love their wives. So let's invite God into our presence and dedicate this hour to Him as we discover how to make love and respect the foundation of our marriages.

"Father God, we thank You for Your abundant love. Thank You for the special gift of marriage. We seek Your presence during our time together. Please show us how we can strengthen our marriages through the values of love and respect. In Your name we pray. Amen."

CONNECTING QUESTION

Before our group watches the video of what Dr. Eggerichs has to share with Mike & Gayle Tucker about love and respect, let's take a moment to connect with each other to share our thoughts about these two values.

Question: Wives, without going into much detail, what is something your husband did recently that communicated to you that he cares about you and loves you deeply? And husbands, very quickly, what is something your wife did recently that communicated to you that she respects you greatly?

SESSION TWO NOTES:

Dr. Eggerichs with Mike & Gayle Tucker

"When that mate loves us, adores us, and respects us, what it does to our souls is without question one of the most gratifying experiences in all of human existence."

Gary Thomas, Devotions for a Sacred Marriage

EXECUTIVE SUMMARY

Love & Respect: Avoiding the Marital Death Spiral

Virtually all problems in a marriage result from a lack of love and respect. Women have the need for love, whereas men have the need for respect. Understanding this fundamental difference between men and women is the first step toward building a healthy and happy marriage that lasts.

The Graveyard Spiral

An off-duty pilot sat beside me the other day on a flight. In our conversation about flying, he started talking about the dreaded "graveyard spiral" that takes the lives of pilots each year (almost all graveyard spirals involve non-instrument rated pilots flying small aircraft).

It is not uncommon for a pilot to encounter poor weather conditions quickly, finding himself engulfed within clouds that prevent visual contact with the horizon or the ground below, making navigation very difficult without instruments. Unable to see the horizon, there is no visual correction for misleading inner-ear cues about which way is up and down.

These sensory illusions can create spatial disorientation that causes the pilot to lose his awareness of altitude. The pilot loses the ability to accurately judge his aircraft's orientation because of his misinterpretation of spatial miscues. With his sense of equilibrium compromised, the plane can be piloted into a tailspin and flown into the ground.

Applying this metaphor to marriage, there are two forces that help to maintain marital equilibrium: Love & Respect. A lack of love and respect creates a poor marital environment that disorients a husband and wife, convincing them that certain things are being said and done for reasons that are not even real or true. This assumption can send their relationship into a "graveyard spiral" that destroys the marriage.

Love & Respect

An environment of love and respect within marriage is the key to a fulfilling relationship and plays a powerful role in raising children who are caring and considerate.

And the Survey Says…

According to Dr. Emerson Eggerichs, love best motivates a woman and respect most powerfully motivates a man. He says, "Research reveals that, during marital conflict, a husband most often reacts when feeling disrespected and a wife reacts when feeling unloved. We asked 7,000 people this question: 'When you are in conflict with your spouse or significant other, do you feel unloved or disrespected?' 83% of the men said 'disrespected.' 72% of the women said 'unloved.' Though we all need love and respect equally, the felt need differs during conflict, and this difference is as different as pink is from blue."

GROUP DISCUSSION

1. Consider this principle: "Respect begets respect." Share examples of how you've seen this principle demonstrated in marriage.

2. If respect begets respect, then does disrespect beget disrespect? If so, share examples of how you've seen this demonstrated in marriage.

3. Read Ephesians 5:33. How does this apply to our culture and marriage today? What is the significance that this counsel comes from God's inspired Word?

4. In the video, we heard about the crazy cycle. When a wife feels unloved, she acts in ways that feel disrespectful to her husband, and when a husband feels disrespected, he acts in ways that feel unloving to his wife. If unaddressed, this behavior can send the marriage into a graveyard spin where, without love, she acts without respect, and without respect, he acts without love, hence the crazy cycle. What are your thoughts about the crazy cycle, and what are some ways to deal with it productively?

5. In what ways have you experienced the pink sunglasses/blue sunglasses effect in your marriage?

6. Dr. Eggerichs says that a husband speaks respect talk and a wife speaks love talk; men speak blue and women speak pink. We must learn some words from each other's vocabulary to have mutual understanding. What are some "pink" words that men might consider using, and some "blue" words women might consider using in conversation?

7. Mutual understanding – not communication – is the key to marriage. How well do you think you and your spouse understand each other?

ASSIGNMENT ONE: CONNECTING WITH YOURSELF

Self-Reflection Questions

Women want to know that they are being loved for who they are as a person and not for their looks or because of what they do or don't do; they want to be valued and loved as a human being.

List three ways that a husband can demonstrate his love for his wife so she knows he loves and values her for who she is as a human being:

1.

2.

3.

Men respond to what they perceive is honorable and fair. When a wife is respectful to her husband in her interactions with him, he will respond in loving and honorable ways.

List three ways that a wife can demonstrate her respect for her husband so he knows she respects him both as a man and as her husband:

1.

2.

3.

ASSIGNMENT TWO: CONNECTING WITH YOUR SPOUSE

It is honorable and fair to talk about a wife's need for love and a husband's need for respect so long as the conversation is not being dismissive, egotistical, narcissistic, or arrogant. Husbands and wives who take time to discuss these issues experience stronger relationships and enjoy happier marriages. The purpose of this activity with your spouse is to get you talking about these two essential needs so you can meet them in more satisfying ways for each other.

About Women

Without love, a wife becomes defensive and reacts offensively toward her husband by showing a lack of respect. She's not trying to be offensive. She is trying to communicate to her husband: "I have a need for love that only you can meet." But her language and tone of voice can become gestures of contempt that send this message to her husband, "I don't respect you." If she's not getting the response she is looking for, a wife will use disrespect to motivate love. Of course, this is ineffective and never works; in fact, it creates the exact opposite effect.

Exercise: Recall the last time this scenario happened in your marriage. What triggered it? Knowing what you know now, what could have been done differently to prevent it from happening? Now that you know what your spouse is really trying to say, what will you do in the future to avoid this situation and help to meet your wife's need for love?

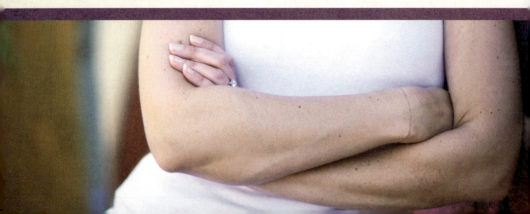

About Men

Without respect, a husband will become defensive and react offensively toward his wife by showing a lack of love. When a man feels provoked, his heart beat increases to more than 100 beats per minute, and he goes into warrior mode. When this shift happens, he realizes that he needs to calm down, which is why a husband tends to withdraw and stonewall. To his wife, this behavior shouts, "I don't love you!" But, he's not trying to say, "I don't love you"; he's saying, "You just said or did something that felt disrespectful to me, so I'm pulling back because that's the honorable thing to do." A husband uses the lack of love – withdrawing – to motivate respect. Of course, this strategy is ineffective and doesn't work; in fact it creates the exact opposite effect.

Exercise: Recall the last time this scenario happened in your marriage. What triggered it? And what could you have done differently to prevent that from happening? Now that you know what your spouse is really trying to say, what will you do in the future to avoid this situation and help to meet your husband's need for respect?

(continued on next page)

Exercise: Decide Now to Create a Safe Marriage Where You Protect Each Other.

For the Husband: When your wife does something that causes you pain, remember that she would never do anything to intentionally harm you. Make this covenant with your wife right now by repeating this promise to her:

"I will always love, respect, and protect you by never doing anything that will intentionally hurt your feelings or harm you in any way."

For the Wife: When your husband does something to hurt you, remember he would never do anything to intentionally harm you. Make this covenant with your husband right now by repeating this promise to him:

"I will always respect, love, and protect you by never doing anything that will intentionally hurt your feelings or harm you in any way."

A New Habit

Having made the above promise to each other, the time has come to put a new communication habit into practice. From now on, when your spouse says or does anything that hurts you, say to him or her:

"What you said or did to me made me feel {insert feeling}, but that couldn't be what you intended because I know you would never intentionally harm me. So, please help me understand what you meant and were trying to say."

CATALYST

Based on what we've learned in session two, here are some reminders, questions, or action steps to get you from where you are to where you want to be, from having a good marriage to having a great marriage. Choose one or two that you will do this week before session three:

1. Remember, contempt does not motivate anyone to change. Words, expressions, and gestures of contempt push your spouse away.

2. Remember, the key to motivating someone to change is meeting that person's deepest need. If you meet a wife's need for love, she's going to be kinder and warmer. And if you meet a man's need for respect, he's going to be kinder and warmer.

3. Stop using rude behavior to trigger love or respect. A wife sometimes acts as if: "If I just show you what's wrong with you, then surely you will straighten up!" A husband sometimes acts as if: "If I'm negative long enough, then surely you will become positive!" Always be kind and loving.

4. Decide to break the crazy cycle of "Without love, she reacts without respect, and without respect, he reacts without love" by choosing to always be loving and respectful no matter what.

5. Read 1 Corinthians 7:33-34 to decode your spouse's truest intention toward you: "But a married man is concerned about the things of the world – how he may please his wife… a married woman is concerned about the things of the world – how she may please her husband." (Holman Christian Standard Bible).

   Choose to understand the lesson being taught: A husband doesn't wake up early in the morning thinking of ways to be unloving to his wife, and a wife doesn't wake up even earlier thinking of ways to be disrespectful to her husband, yet it seems this way when we feel unloved and disrespected.

6. Decode the basic goodwill that's hidden in the response of your spouse by asking yourself these next two questions.

   Question one: Is my wife acting this way because she is trying to be disrespectful or because she's saying, "I have a need that only you can meet"? Ultimately, you could see it as a compliment, because what she's really saying is that you and you alone, as her husband, can meet her deepest need for love – and she's coming to YOU for that need to be satisfied.

   Question two: Is my husband reacting this way because he is trying to be unloving or because he's saying, "I have a need for respect that only you can meet"? Ultimately, you could see it as a compliment, because what he's really saying is that you and you alone, as his wife, can meet his deepest need for respect – and he's coming to YOU for that need to be satisfied."

7. What are three ways you would like for your husband to demonstrate his love for you this week:

   1.

   2.

   3.

8. List three ways you can show respect for your husband this week:

   1.

   2.

   3.

(Catalyst continued)

9. What are three ways you would like for your wife to demonstrate her respect for you this week:

    1.

    2.

    3.

10. List three ways you can show love for your wife this week:

    1.

    2.

    3.

RESOURCES

§ *The Love She Most Desires; The Respect He Desperately Needs*, Dr. Emerson Eggerichs

§ www.LoveAndRespect.com

NEXT WEEK, SESSION THREE

Forgiveness: Healing Love's Deepest Wounds

Human beings hurt one another intentionally and unintentionally. Even within marriage, we say or do hurtful things to the one we love most – to the very person we would never ever think of hurting because we cherish them so deeply, to the point of sacrificing our own lives for them if needed. But harsh words and thoughtless actions leave emotional and spiritual scars, sometimes even bruised bodies in the most extreme situations. There is a pathway to happiness and to being madly in love again… and that pathway is called forgiveness.

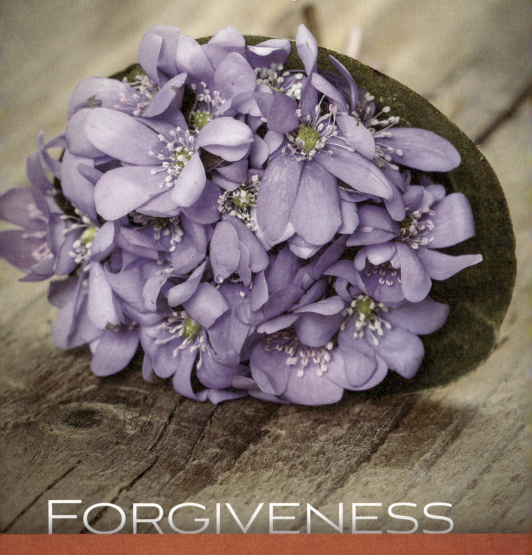

SESSION 3

FORGIVENESS

HEALING LOVE'S DEEPEST WOUNDS

*"The weak can never forgive.
Forgiveness is the attribute of the strong."*
~ MAHATMA GANDHI

What You Will Discover in Session Three

In session three, you will meet Dan B. Allender, Ph.D., author of numerous books and Professor of Counseling at the Seattle School of Theology & Psychology in Seattle, Washington, and you will also meet Dr. Tremper Longman, Professor of Biblical Studies at Westmont College in Santa Barbara, California.

A failure to forgive prevents a husband or wife from having an open heart that gives and receives love and also from experiencing the sweet joy of emotional, mental, spiritual, and physical intimacy. In this session, we will discover how to begin the forgiveness process in our marriage so we can be/stay madly in love for the rest of our lives.

Opening Prayer

The Bible says in Psalm 103:10-12 that God treats us with love and compassion despite our failures and shortcomings, and that as far as the east is from the west, He removes our sins from us. God is the author of the second chance (and the third and fourth and fifth chances, too). His forgiveness is amazing and complete, and it restores our relationship with Him.

Let's invite God into our presence so that His life-transforming grace may be alive in our lives and marriages.

"Father God, Your love is so radical and amazing. Thank You for loving us so much. Thank You for your forgiveness that heals and restores our lives. May Your grace melt our hearts so we become husbands and wives who overflow with forgiveness, just like You. In Your name we pray. Amen."

CONNECTING QUESTION

Before we watch the video of Drs. Allender and Longman sharing their thoughts on forgiveness and its role in marriage, let's connect with each other to see where we are as a group with this concept and practice of forgiveness.

Question: What impact, if any, does a refusal to forgive have on a marriage – and what are some results of failing to forgive?

SESSION THREE NOTES:

Drs. Allender & Longman with Mike & Gayle Tucker

You must deal with your own sin and forgive yourself 1st before you deal with the other person.
1) Forgive self 1st then others
2) It (lack of forgiveness) if harbored will literally tear the body down.

> "Resist becoming offended at every little thing your spouse says/does. Let the love of God in your heart suffocate the offense."
>
> Marriage Works! Blog Post

EXECUTIVE SUMMARY

FORGIVENESS: HEALING LOVE'S DEEPEST WOUNDS

The truth is that, even though we don't want to, sometimes we hurt those whom we love most. There isn't one of us who can live our lives in a marriage without hurting our spouse at some point, either intentionally or unintentionally. And when we hurt our husband or wife, we have two choices: 1) End the relationship, or 2) Find a way to forgive and be forgiven so our hearts can be healed and restored.

THE PROBLEM WITH FORGIVENESS

Forgiveness is difficult. When our heart is wounded, we withdraw our love because we don't want to be hurt again.

Forgiveness is so difficult within marriage because, in one sense, it is the very hardest part of what it means to love. You really can't love unless your heart risks getting hurt and is willing to forgive. But the very nature of forgiveness means that I am literally willing to receive back into my arms the very person who hurt me. That is not an easy decision or process!

One of the most difficult things in the world is to open your heart again to the person who hurt you and love them fully again.

Marriage seems to magnify our sins and hurts against each another. Our relationship with our husband or wife reveals not only our great and wonderful potential to love, but also our human weaknesses and shortcomings as a person and as a spouse.

One of the many purposes God has for marriage is for it to be a kind of mirror, revealing how far we have fallen from His quality and standard of love.

And yet, on the other hand, marriage is the very context that gives us the sweetest taste of what heaven holds and what love can be. And although this may sound confusing and somewhat contradictory, marriage can be a taste of hell – an environment of separation and death of love – or it can be the sweetest taste of heaven and the most intimate, abundant, and passionate love we will ever know this side of heaven.

Forgiveness is the key.

GROUP DISCUSSION

1. Two Core Convictions/Experiences:
   Dr. Allender suggests that the two core contexts of marriage we all experience are the context of suffering – learning how to suffer – and the context of experiencing the sweetest notions of God's love. Share what this idea means to you and for your marriage.

2. The context of suffering within marriage "unearths something of that mess within us." What is the "mess" Dr. Allender speaks of? What has been your experience with it in marriage?

3. How is it possible for us to "taste" a certain kind of pain in marriage that we don't experience in other relationships in quite the same way?

4. How does the context of pain and suffering in marriage reveal that we don't "do" forgiveness well, and how does it teach and encourage a husband and wife to grow together as a couple?

5. Why are we reluctant to forgive sometimes?

6. Why should we be willing to engage the process of forgiveness?

7. How does being forgiven by God personally relate to our willingness to forgive our spouse?

8. What are the end results of choosing to not forgive our spouse?

9. What are the effects and outcomes of choosing to forgive our spouse?

10. What does the concept of forgiveness "covering our shame" mean to you? And how does it feel knowing that by forgiving your spouse you can give them "new clothes" and cover their shame?

ASSIGNMENT ONE: CONNECTING WITH YOURSELF

Self-Reflection Questions

(For this session, Mike & Gayle strongly urge you to find a place where you can be alone because these exercises may stir strong emotions within you. Find a safe, comfortable place where you can be yourself. You may also consider taking along inspiring music to comfort you as you journal your thoughts).

You are a human being who has been, as the Bible says, fearfully and wonderfully made in the image of God. But with that being said, you're human, too, which means that along with a great capacity to love there is an equal capacity to hurt and be hurt.

List two instances when you felt deeply wounded by your spouse:

1.

2.

Now, list two instances when you know that you said or did something (or didn't say or do something that you should have) that deeply wounded your spouse:

1.

2.

One of the first steps of the healing process is receiving God's forgiveness. The Bible offers this promise in 1 John 1:9, "If we confess our sins, He is faithful and just and will forgive us our sins and purify us from all unrighteousness" (New International Standard Version).

What is something for which you would like to ask God's forgiveness? He is waiting…all you have to do is ask…so ask now.

What is something for which you know you need to forgive your spouse? If you persist in withholding your forgiveness, what will happen to your marriage? In fact, how is failing to forgive affecting your relationship now? Forgiveness is a choice. Will you choose to open your heart and arms to your spouse once more through the process of forgiveness?

ASSIGNMENT TWO: CONNECTING WITH YOUR SPOUSE

The Bible says that, while we were yet sinners, Jesus died for us and forgave our sins. While we were still in the act and process of hurting Him, He opened His heart and arms to not only receive us into His life again, but to keep us in His life forever through His wonderful gift of eternal grace.

In a kind, caring, and loving spirit, discuss the following questions together:

1. If the grace of Jesus Christ can heal our hearts and transform our lives individually, then what can His grace do for our marriage and the life we share as husband and wife?

2. How has a lack of forgiveness affected your marriage? In which direction is a lack of forgiveness pushing your relationship, and is this the direction you want your marriage to go?

3. If it is safe and productive, consider sharing what you listed as instances that you wounded your spouse and felt wounded by them.

4. As a result of what you have learned in this session, please share what the forgiveness process means to you and what you expect from it.

5. Each of us has imperfections. From the perspective of an imperfect spouse with faults and shortcomings, does knowing that you are also a sinner affect the expectations you have of your spouse? And what impact does it have on the forgiveness process – does it make you more gracious, compassionate, patient, and understanding?

6. We started this session by saying forgiveness is one of the most difficult things in a marriage because we are opening our heart and arms to receiving the very person who wounded us so deeply. Are you willing to receive and offer forgiveness to begin the process of healing your relationship with your spouse? If so, then hold hands and ask for each other's forgiveness, and then seal your decision with prayer. You may offer your own prayer or pray the one Mike & Gayle have written for you:

"Dear Heavenly Father, thank You for Your love and forgiveness. Please be alive in our marriage. We seek Your grace and strength for a healthy & happy relationship. Thank You for a fresh start and a new beginning. Thank You, too, for this amazing person that I get to share the rest of my life with. Your love is amazing – and it makes the love we share with You and each other amazing, too. In Your name we pray. Amen."

CATALYST

Based on what we've learned in session three, here are some reminders, questions, or action steps to get you from where you are to where you want to be, from having a good marriage to having a great marriage. Choose one or two to focus on this week before session four.

1. Remember that everyone, including you, is an imperfect human being with flaws and shortcomings.

2. Withholding forgiveness harms your marriage and damages your well-being. You deserve the benefits that come from offering forgiveness.

3. Someone doesn't have to repent or say they're sorry for you to forgive them. So forgive and let go – even if you don't think they deserve it; maybe they don't, but you do.

4. Remember, refusing to forgive, or requiring someone to repent or say they're sorry, perpetuates damage and victimization.

5. Always deal with yourself first spiritually when it comes to forgiveness before "dealing" with your spouse; it will make you kinder, merciful, and likelier to forgive.

6. What does it mean to you and your marriage to realize that forgiveness is a supernatural act that comes from God?

7. Forgiveness is a process that brings healing and restoration.

8. Forgiveness and mercy are not just reserved for the "big" hurts that happen in marriage, but are for the little everyday hurts, too. Compassion, kindness, patience, forgiveness, and love are habits of love.

9. Forgiveness isn't a burden; it's one of life's greatest pleasures we can possibly know. It creates a kind of thanksgiving feast where we can enjoy the bountiful abundance of love. Therefore, we see forgiveness as the greatest gift we can give to one another.

10. The next time your spouse hurts you, consider doing this in a spirit of love and reconciliation. Say to him or her: "I don't know if you realize it, but what you did hurt me. I am going to assume that you were unaware, but it has made me feel _____. Would you be willing to talk about it?"

RESOURCES

§ *The Healing Path: How the Hurts in Your Past Can Lead You to a More Abundant Life*, Dan B. Allender, Ph.D.

§ www.ThePathLessChosen.com (Dr. Allender's website)

§ *Forgiveness (Intimate Marriage)*, by Dr. Tremper Longman

NEXT WEEK, SESSION FOUR

Marriage Myths: Damaging Myths About Relationships

In session four, we will dispel 10 of the most common relationship myths that are trapping couples within a quicksand of madness. You can be in love AND also like your spouse at the same time! Join us next week to break free from the 10 myths that could be strangling your love.

SESSION 4

MARRIAGE MYTHS

DAMAGING MYTHS ABOUT RELATIONSHIPS

*"Don't marry the person you think you can live with;
marry only the individual you think you can't live without."*

~ JAMES DOBSON ~

What You Will Discover in Session Four

In session four, you will meet marriage and family therapist Dr. Linda Mintle, author of *I Married You, Not Your Family, and Nine Other Relationship Myths That Can Ruin Your Marriage*. Dr. Mintle joins Mike & Gayle Tucker to dispel the 10 most common relationship myths that keep couples from being madly in love.

Opening Prayer

Every relationship has more than its fair share of conflict and difficulty. And it doesn't take long after the honeymoon is over for a husband and wife to realize that marriage isn't always fun or easy. But with an unwavering commitment to each other, and God's guidance and grace, they can navigate relational hazards to stay madly in love.

What we really need when dealing with relationship myths is truth, because the Bible promises us that the truth will set us free. So, let's pause a moment to invite God's presence into our midst so we are guided by His Divine Wisdom.

"Father God, we invite You to be in our group today as we spend this special time together. Please guide our thoughts and discussion so Your truth will free us from any myths or illusions that are harming our marriages. In Your name we pray. Amen."

CONNECTING QUESTION

Before we watch the video to learn what Dr. Mintle has to say about marriage myths, let's consider some of our own perceptions.

Question: Do you think it's possible to live happily ever after? Or is it an idealistic fantasy made popular in books and movies?

SESSION FOUR NOTES:

Dr. Mintle with Mike & Gayle Tucker

Be open to "I may be part of the problem"

Remember All <u>all</u> marriages are under spiritual attack.

Your whole family too! I thought I married only you!

"Love is blind, but marriage is a real eye opener."

Anonymous

Executive Summary

Marriage Myths: Damaging Myths About Relationships

Couples are divorcing every day over fixable problems that stem from marriage myths that are ruining their love.

But when eyes are opened to the truth behind some of the most maddening conflicts and frustrations, couples see that many of their beliefs about marriage are rooted in fiction and not in fact.

If they can handle the truth about themselves and their marriage, they will become better husbands and wives and find the power to create the kind of marriage they have always dreamed of having.

Uncomfortable Truths

The freedom that truth offers is absolutely wonderful, but it can be a bittersweet process. We don't always want to hear what needs to be heard, such as:

1. The truth that we might be part of the problem. Next time you catch yourself saying or thinking, If only she would… or I wish he would, take a few moments to consider your role in the situation.

2. Another difficult truth to come to terms with is this one: The only person I can change is myself. Manipulation, begging, nagging, coercing, threatening, or bribing do not work. Change comes from within and not from without. My marriage will change when I change.

3. Here is another tough one: My behavior is affecting how my spouse responds to me, and it is influencing my marriage for better or worse every day.

4. So many couples overlook this next truth: Our marriages are under attack by the unseen principalities and powers of this world that the Bible talks about. Just as there are mental, physical, and emotional aspects to a marriage, there is a spiritual aspect, too. So when a husband and wife fall out of spiritual oneness with one another and God, they open their marriage to attack. Without God's presence in the relationship, it becomes very difficult to treat each other with mutual love, respect, and forgiveness. The spiritual dimension creates a heavenly environment, if you will, and connects them to a greater purpose.

GROUP DISCUSSION

The Ten Marriage Myths
(Note: Discuss two or three myths, as time permits)

1. **Myth: Marriage is a Contract.**
   Truth: Marriage is a covenant designed by God. It's absolutely true that we sign a contract when we get married. Contracts carry the idea that you give me what I want or need, and if I get enough of what I want or need, then I will stay in this relationship with you. In America, if we don't get what we want, we end the contract and leave. But marriage isn't based on a contract; it's based on a covenant – an unbreakable promise. What does the contract versus covenant concept mean to you? And how is a marriage bound by covenant different than one bound by contract?

2. **Myth: I Married You, Not Your Family!**
   Truth: You don't just marry your spouse. You get the package deal. The way we deal with anger and conflict is typically based on what we saw our parents model. It's helpful to understand that our spouse brings their world and all of that history – everything they saw modeled growing up in their home – with them into our marriage, because it's part of who they are. Family dynamics are a big deal. Share how family dynamics have affected your marriage.

3. **Myth: I Can Change My Spouse.**
   Truth: You can only change yourself. God didn't create us with the power to change another human being. We can influence, but not change. The video stated that, "You cannot change another person, but you can change your reaction to that person. And, as a result, it changes the relationship." What does this mean? And how does keeping the focus on changing yourself prevent manipulation?

4. **Myth: We Are Too Different – Irreconcilable Differences.**
   Truth: Incompatibilities or differences don't destroy a relationship. It's how you work through your differences that counts.
   <u>Differences are healthy when they're not differences in values.</u>
   When people with differences in values marry, they face many more challenges. How they work through their differences, and the conflict resolution style they use, determines the outcome of their marriage. How do you handle differences in your marriage?

5. **Myth: I've Lost That Loving Feeling, and it's Gone, Gone, Gone!**
   Truth: That loving feeling can be restored. Losing that loving feeling, as the song goes, is one of the main reasons why people divorce.

   The road to lost love begins with:

   § Criticism. You start finding problems with your spouse. You nit-pick and react negatively. This escalates to:

   § Feelings of contempt. You begin feeling that you don't like your spouse and would rather not be around them. Which leads to:

   § Feelings of defensiveness. This results in:

   § Stonewalling. This creates emotional distance.

   Emotional distance is the number one predictor of divorce.
   Based on what we have learned so far in this Mad About Marriage small group series, what are some tools for dealing with emotional distance? And what are some ways we can create a safe haven in our marriage to help protect our partners and ourselves from the unnecessary pain of wounding each other? How can loving feelings be restored?

6. **Myth: A More Traditional Marriage (e.g. 1950s) Will Save Our Relationship.**
   Truth: God's intention is gender equality; a more traditional marriage will save our marriage. Sometimes, people think that if the wife just stayed home, or if things were like they were in the 1950s, then things would be much better. Truth is, times have changed. But even though it's the 21st century, we can still cherish and practice the values of mutual love and respect. How might a "traditional" marriage function in modern times?

7. **Myth: I Can't Change Who I Am – Take it or Leave it.**
   Truth: I can change, but it requires desire, obedience, and God's power. This whole notion of, "You knew this was the way I was when you married me, so take it or leave it," is a cop out. Transformation is the hallmark of God's faithful presence operating within our lives. The power to change is within us because the power of the Holy Spirit resides within. Anything is possible with faith, God's grace, and the power of choice. How should one's personal transformation affect a marriage?

8. **Myth: There's Been an Affair, so We Need to Get a Divorce.**
   Truth: Affairs break trust and cause deep pain, but reconciliation is possible. The road to healing and recovery from an affair isn't an impossible road. God's grace and forgiveness enable us to overcome betrayal. Yes, it is a very difficult process for couples to go through. But with time, trust can be restored and the marriage healed. Forgiving someone isn't condoning adultery. What are some ways a couple may heal their marriage after emotional or physical infidelity has occurred?

9. **Myth: It Doesn't Matter What I Do – I Can Live However I Wish. Cheap Grace.**
   Truth: Receive God's grace and have a repentant heart.
   God's grace doesn't give us a license to hurt our spouse. Just because we know God forgives us doesn't give us the right to cause our husband or wife pain. We have a responsibility, to ourselves and to our partner, to grow and develop and become a better person – the kind of person our spouse can trust and knows will never harm them. What can we do to make sure we don't take our spouse's love for granted and presume he or she will forgive us?

10. **Myth: It's Too Broken. Nothing Can Fix This Relationship.**
    Truth: It's never too late, because nothing is impossible with God. Nothing is impossible. Just as we learned in session one, your marriage is good enough to save. With time, patience, and a commitment to do whatever it takes, you can restore your relationship and be madly in love again. Why do people give up on a marriage that is good enough to save? What are one or two key things they can do to try to save their marriage and make things work?

ASSIGNMENT ONE: CONNECTING WITH YOURSELF

Self-Reflection Questions

1. Review the 10 myths. Which of them has been "true" for you, either currently or in the past?

2. Which of the 10 myths, if any, have been undermining your marriage?

3. Cancel your myths by writing your own truth. For any myth that used to be true for you, state your new truth. For example:

   "I used to think that I couldn't change who I am – that my spouse had to take it or leave it. But the truth I now hold dear in my heart is that, by God's grace and strength, and the power of choice that He gives me, I can choose to transform my life."

   Cancel your myths by rewriting your new truth in your own words.

ASSIGNMENT TWO: CONNECTING WITH YOUR SPOUSE

Find a comfortable environment you both enjoy, without interruptions or distractions. You need to be fully present and supportive of each other emotionally and spiritually. It is essential for you to create a safe haven for this assignment because you might feel exposed and vulnerable. In fact, as you begin, promise each other you will be kind and loving and will refrain from doing anything that would harm, diminish, or embarrass the other.

Discuss the Following:

1. Evaluate the foundation of your marriage. Is your relationship based more on a contract or on a covenant? Which do you want it to be? How will committing yourself to an unbreakable promise impact your relationship and marriage from this day forward?

2. Share with your spouse which, if any, of the 10 myths used to be true for you before learning the "real" truth about them.

3. What are two or three myths you think might have been undermining your love for each other – and what will you do to restore truth to your marriage?

4. Consider buying Dr. Linda Mintle's book, *I Married You, Not Your Family, and Nine Other Relationship Myths That Can Ruin Your Marriage*, and read a chapter each week together for a happier marriage.

CATALYST

This section is a quick summary of the 10 myths. You might want to make a copy of this page and keep it with you. Circle the myths you want to get rid of that have been undermining your marriage. Whenever you catch yourself falling for one of them in the coming days and weeks, stop and read the "real" truth about the matter to refocus and support your new decision – your "new" truth.

1. **Myth: Marriage is a Contract.**
   Truth: Marriage is a covenant designed by God.

2. **Myth: I Married You, Not Your Family!**
   Truth: You don't just marry your spouse. You get the package deal.

3. **Myth: I Can Change My Spouse.**
   Truth: I can only change myself.

4. **Myth: We Are Too Different – Our Differences Are Irreconcilable.**
   Truth: Incompatibilities or differences don't destroy a relationship. It's how we work through our differences that counts.

5. **Myth: I've Lost That Loving Feeling, and its Gone, Gone, Gone!**
   Truth: That loving feeling can be restored.

6. **Myth: A More Traditional Marriage (e.g. 1950s) Will Save Our Relationship.**
   Truth: God's intention is gender equality; a more traditional marriage will save us.

7. **Myth: I Can't Change Who I Am – Take it or Leave it.**
   Truth: I can change who I am if I have desire, obedience, and God's power.

8. **Myth: There's Been an Affair, So We Need to Get a Divorce.**
   Truth: Affairs break trust and cause deep pain, but reconciliation is possible.

9. **Myth: It Doesn't Matter What I Do – I Can Live However I Wish. Cheap Grace.**
   Truth: I receive God's grace and power to transform my life.

10. **Myth: It's Too Broken. Nothing Can Fix This Marriage.**
    Truth: It's never too late, because nothing is impossible with God.

RESOURCES

§ *I Married You, Not Your Family, and Nine Other Relationship Myths That Can Ruin Your Marriage*, Dr. Linda Mintle

§ www.DrLindaHelps.com

NEXT WEEK, SESSION FIVE

Intimacy & Desire: Getting That Loving Feeling Back!

Couples who enjoy frequent sexual intimacy are healthier, happier, and more satisfied with each other. Next week, we will learn ways to improve and enhance emotional intimacy within our marriages so we can be madly in love sexually, too!

SESSION 5

Privacy Please

INTIMACY & DESIRE

GETTING THAT LOVING FEELING BACK!

"I don't understand couples who say they are too busy or too tired to sleep together. Unless they are building roads all day or running a multinational corporation, I expect they have just lost sight of priorities."

— BARBARA "CUTIE" COOPER

What You Will Discover in Session Five

In session five, we will meet Dr. David Schnarch, who is an author, a licensed clinical psychologist, and the Director of the Marriage and Family Health Center in Evergreen, Colorado. Dr. Schnarch will help us tackle the tough issue of why there is such a low level of intimacy in marriages today and explore the relationship between spirituality and sex.

Opening Prayer

God created sexual intimacy to be enjoyed within the sacred union of marriage, where two people become one flesh and build a life together. This isn't a topic we should avoid or be embarrassed of. Sex is a wonderful, exciting gift when enjoyed the way God intended. So let's pray and seek His blessing as we discuss one of the most misunderstood issues in marriage today.

"Father God, thank You for Your love and the wonderful gift of marriage. We're exploring a topic in this session that can make people uncomfortable. But we know it's something we need to talk about. So please lead and guide our discussion today. May we grow in the emotional and physical intimacy that You have planned for us. In Your name we pray. Amen."

CONNECTING QUESTION

Before we watch the video to learn what Dr. David Schnarch has to say about emotional and sexual intimacy, here's a question for you.

Question: How common are emotional and sexual problems in marriages today?

SESSION FIVE NOTES:

Dr. David Schnarch with Mike & Gayle Tucker

"I think that marriage is an elegant people-growing machine with the kind of sophistication that really reveals the handiwork of the Divine."

Dr. David Schnarch

EXECUTIVE SUMMARY
INTIMACY & DESIRE: GETTING THAT LOVING FEELING BACK!

According to research, couples with the healthiest and happiest marriages are those who have frequent sexual intimacy. But it isn't as simple as deciding to have more sex so you can have a better marriage. Physical intimacy is a byproduct of emotional intimacy.

Sadly, many marriages today are void of emotional intimacy, which explains why an increasing number of husbands and wives co-exist in celibate marriages.

Dr. Schnarch has had more than 18,000 people participate in a study on sexual intimacy found at **Crucible4Points.com**. Here are the shocking results:

§   Of the 18,000 people, half say their sex life is either dead or dying

§   25% say their sex life is asleep and needs a wake-up call

§   Only 25% say their sex life is alive and well

§   85% of people report having sexual desire problems either sometimes, always, or virtually every time they have sex

Don't feel bad, guilty, or ashamed if you and your spouse have difficulty in this area; you are not alone.

In a nation of people who appear to be obsessed with sex and having sex, it seems that many couples are not enjoying sex. The media paints a steamy picture of what is happening in bedrooms throughout this country, but in reality, the bedroom has become one of the coldest, loneliest places in America.

In this session, we will discover how emotionally committed husbands and wives interact with each other. We will also explore the spiritual dimension of physical intimacy, because God meant for sex to include a spiritual element, too.

Here is the good news: Emotional and sexual intimacy can be reclaimed. Even if your relationship has been facing challenges to emotional and physical intimacy, resulting in low desire and minimal sexual frequency, there is still great hope for your marriage. You can transform your bedroom from a place of loneliness and isolation into a place of amazing passion and intimacy that ignites your marriage with profound joy.

GROUP DISCUSSION

1. After seeing the video, what are your thoughts about couples struggling with emotional and sexual intimacy, and coexisting in celibate marriages?

2. Dr. Schnarch says that sexual intimacy "Tests our spirituality, because if you really want to see what people believe about the face of God, then I think it really shows up with what happens in the bedroom." What does this mean to you, and how does it apply to marriage?

3. Discuss these comments by Dr. Schnarch from the video: "You can badger your partner into having sex, but you can't badger your partner into wanting you. And, so, respecting each other is a very important thing, and it's why a lot of couples don't have sex – they've stopped respecting each other."

"They (husbands and wives) are dependent upon each other for validation. And human beings don't like having sex with people who they have to prop up emotionally. And, so, in dealing with those kinds of things in marriage, all of a sudden, you realize that sex is not something in marriage; sex is one of the drive wheels of marriage, not because we all want to have sex, but because of our personhood – becoming a human being is wired into sex. So many people have difficulty with sex because they got married and NEVER expected they would have to grow, and if you stop growing, then your sex and intimacy isn't going to be worth having, which is why a lot of people don't have sex."

4. Let's talk about the Quiet Mind Calm Heart concept, which is having the ability to control our emotions and sooth our own hearts so that we are emotionally autonomous. People who cannot control themselves tend to try to control the people around them. Learning how to control our own emotions allows people around us to live their own lives. How is this relevant to personhood, to emotional and sexual intimacy, and to the frequency of sex?

5. Another concept Dr. Schnarch shared was Grounded Responding, which he describes as:

    § The ability to not overreact to things, AND

    § Pushing ourselves to deal with issues, such as sexual problems, that we often avoid.

    Give examples of the Grounded Responding concept.

6. What are your thoughts and feelings about the ten-minute hug as a tool to rewire the brain for emotional intimacy? What are different ways of doing the ten-minute hug?

ASSIGNMENT ONE: CONNECTING WITH YOURSELF

SELF-REFLECTION QUESTIONS

Do you feel satisfied or dissatisfied with the quality of the emotional and sexual intimacy of your marriage? Are you satisfied or dissatisfied with the frequency of sex? If you are dissatisfied, then, based on what you have learned in this session, what are some reasons why this might be the case? What are two or three things you can do to increase the emotional and sexual intimacy of your marriage?

There are two sides to the Quiet Mind Calm Heart concept that we learned about this week: 1) one has to do with a spouse who needs to be propped up emotionally; 2) the other involves a spouse who controls other people because he or she is unable to control his or her own emotions. Has either of these issues affected your marriage? What can you do to grow in these areas personally and in your marriage?

Dr. Schnarch discussed the four points of balance that support spirituality and enhance emotional and sexual intimacy and frequency of sex. They are:

1. **A Solid, Flexible Self**

    The solid, flexible self is about having a set of core values that transcend circumstances and difficult times. But it's also about being flexible and adaptable, because rigidity is unhealthy to marriage. (Rigid faith is unhealthy, too.)

    What are some values that anchor you during difficult times? Would your spouse describe you as 'rigid' or 'flexible'?

2. **A Quiet Mind and a Calm Heart**

    We've already discussed how having a quiet mind and calm heart is the ability to be in charge of our emotions so our spouse doesn't have to prop us up, and that it is also the ability to control ourselves and not feel the need to control others. Be kind to yourself, but answer honestly:

    1. To what degree do you struggle with needing someone to prop you up emotionally?

    2. To what degree do you try to control others because you struggle with controlling yourself?

3. **GROUNDED RESPONDING**

    Grounded responding is the ability to not overreact and to take the initiative to address problems. Are there issues in your marriage to which you tend to overreact? Are there any problems you've been avoiding that you know in your heart you need to address?

4. **MEANINGFUL ENDURANCE**

    Meaningful endurance is the ability and willingness to persevere through difficulty, to handle failure in healthy ways, and to keep going. It involves committing to dealing with difficult issues in order to succeed. Every couple with sexual desire problems will need to practice meaningful endurance. Are you committed to persevering through your problems with the intention of healing your relationship with your spouse and making your marriage better?

The Ten-Minute Hug Explained

The ten-minute hug is a special tool couples can use to establish deeper connection. In this exercise, the couple lies down on the bed, facing each other, (keeping their clothes on, if they prefer). They lay their heads on their pillows and gaze into one another's eyes for 10 minutes, allowing themselves to become calm as they tune into each other. If the couple feels like touching, they hold hands – nothing more.

Experiencing The Ten-Minute Hug

This exercise may feel uncomfortable at first, especially if there has been a lack of physical or emotional intimacy, but it has great power to create connection between you and your spouse. There are cells in the back of your brain that are stimulated only when you look into the eyes of another person. Trust that this process will begin rewiring your brain and healing your heart. Most people find themselves relaxing and growing calmer as the minutes pass.

Consider your willingness to engage in the ten-minute hug. While it may seem awkward or risky, the growth in connection and intimacy will be incredibly rewarding and well worth the emotional investment.

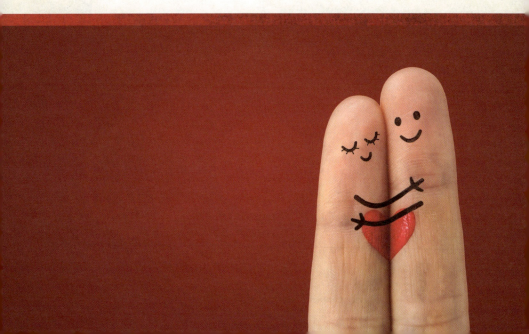

ASSIGNMENT TWO: CONNECTING WITH YOUR SPOUSE

Find a comfortable, distraction-free place. If you are restoring emotional and sexual intimacy to your marriage, and you have been distant from each other, you might feel vulnerable. This response is natural. Offer your love and support to each other as you embark upon this journey together. Promise to listen to each other and accept one another with unconditional love. Refrain from saying or doing anything that would harm your spouse emotionally.

1. Share your thoughts and decisions about what you learned from the Connecting With Yourself assignment. If you have not completed that assignment, do it now before continuing.

2. Discuss the four points of balance and how you would like for them to function within your marriage:

   1. A solid flexible self
   2. A quiet mind and a calm heart
   3. Grounded responding
   4. Meaningful endurance

3. Review the following statements by Dr. Schnarch and discuss what relevance, if any, they will have on your marriage moving forward:

   "You can badger your partner into having sex, but you can't badger your partner into wanting you. So, respecting each other is a very important thing. That's why a lot of couples don't have sex – they've stopped respecting each other."

"They (husbands and wives) are dependent upon each other for validation. Human beings don't like having sex with people whom they have to prop up emotionally; so, in dealing with those kinds of things in marriage, all of a sudden, you realize that sex is not something *in* marriage; sex is one of the drive wheels *of* marriage, not because we all want to have sex, *but because of our personhood.* Becoming a human being is wired into sex. So many people have difficulty with sex because they got married and NEVER expected they would have to grow. If you stop growing, then your sex and intimacy isn't going to be worth having, which is why a lot of people don't have sex."

4. Finally, use the tool of the ten-minute hug to begin the process of rekindling your emotional and physical intimacy. Experience the ten-minute hug: Lie down beside each other on the bed (keeping your clothes on, if you prefer). Lay your heads on your pillows, facing one another. Give yourselves a few minutes to calm down, because you may feel uncomfortable at first if you've not been physically intimate or lack emotional intimacy. If you feel like touching your partner, then only hold hands – nothing more. Allow yourselves to become calm as you tune into each other and gaze into one another's eyes. There are cells in the back of your brain that light up only when you look into another person's eyes, so trust that this process will begin rewiring your brain and healing your heart. You will find yourself relaxing and growing calmer as the minutes pass. The ten-minute hug is a special tool you and your spouse can use to establish deeper connection.

CATALYST

Based on what we've learned in session five, here are some reminders, questions, or action steps to get you from where you are to where you want to be, from having a good marriage to having a great marriage. Choose one or two to focus on this week before session six.

1. Remember, the same tools that help a couple repair sex and intimacy in marriage are the exact ones you need to be an amazing parent or to survive an economic downturn. The four points of balance are tools for successful living.

2. Learn to use the four points of balance as tools for spiritual growth, too. Authentic spirituality is about having a solid, flexible self and being able to handle our own emotions. (Taking care of ourselves emotionally is a gift from God). Authentic spirituality is also about not overreacting or needing to be propped up, persevering through the tough times, and being willing to address problems.

3. Consider this amazing benefit of marriage: "Marriage is an elegant people-growing machine with the kind of sophistication that reveals the handiwork of the Divine."
– Dr. David Schnarch

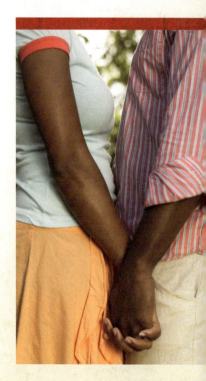

4. Decide daily to have an emotionally committed relationship with your spouse.

5. Respect and love your spouse.

6. Validate and affirm your spouse.

7. Remember that sex isn't just something in marriage, but a drive wheel of marriage.

8. Remember, emotional and sexual intimacy are ways to experience personhood.

9. Find ways to strengthen your collaborative alliance with your partner.

10. Love your spouse unconditionally.

RESOURCES

§ *Intimacy and Desire: Awaken the Passion In Your Marriage,* Dr. David Schnarch

§ *www.Crucible4Points.com*

NEXT WEEK, SESSION SIX

Commitment: Living Happily Ever After

In session six, we will explore how to maintain a strong marriage, and what it takes to live happily ever after.

SESSION 6

COMMITMENT

LIVING HAPPILY EVER AFTER

"Let the wife make the husband glad to come home,
and let him make her sorry to see him leave."

— MARTIN LUTHER

What You Will Discover in Session Six

In session six, we will once again hear from Willie and Elaine Oliver, directors of the Department of Family Ministries at the Seventh-Day Adventist Church in Silver Spring, Maryland, about what real commitment in marriage looks like and how we can live happily ever after with our spouse.

Opening Prayer

God is trustworthy and faithful; He is committed to us and to the happiness of our marriages. He knows our relationship struggles, hurts, and joys. But as the Author of love, He also knows how to heal our hearts and fill our marriages with joy so we may live happily ever after. So let's take a moment to invite Him into our presence as we study what commitment really means.

"Father God, great is Your faithfulness and commitment to us. Show us what true commitment in marriage looks like so we can be faithful to our spouses and live happily ever after. In Your name we pray. Amen."

CONNECTING QUESTION

Before we watch the video to learn what Willie and Elaine Oliver teach about the true nature of commitment, consider this question.

Question: How committed do you think couples really are to each other today?

SESSION SIX NOTES:

WILLIE AND ELAINE OLIVER WITH MIKE & GAYLE TUCKER

"When people get married because they think it's a long-time love affair, they'll be divorced very soon, because all love affairs end in disappointment. But marriage is a recognition of a spiritual identity."

JOSEPH CAMPBELL

EXECUTIVE SUMMARY

COMMITMENT: LIVING HAPPILY EVER AFTER

Every marriage goes through difficult times. Couples struggle over issues from their past, financial problems, in-law difficulties, experiences of loss and grief, or just the natural problems of two imperfect people learning to live as one.

When problems arise, and they will, what gets couples through difficult times? What makes it possible for the marriage to survive and grow into a rich and fulfilling relationship yielding a lifetime of happiness?

COMMITMENT.

But not the kind of "business contract" commitment we see modeled in our society today.

Couples who enter marriage with a business contract mentality are setting themselves up for failure. Why? Because they are already thinking about how to end the relationship when something goes wrong or doesn't work out.

When you enter marriage as a business contract, then you have what are called "deal breakers." These are actions or behaviors that are considered to be a breach of contract.

Authentic commitment doesn't have an escape clause. True commitment looks like this: Divorce is not an option.

The Bible says that marital commitment is a covenant. A covenant is different than a contract. A contract says, "I love me, but I like you" or "Because I love me, I want you to do so-and-so for me."

A covenant says this: "I love you – not only because of what you do for me, but I love you because I promised to love you."

So, a covenant isn't about what your spouse has done for you lately, or even satisfying your expectations by doing everything perfectly. A covenant is about choice: "I love you because I *decided* to love you, and I *promised* to love you unconditionally." This removes the emphasis regarding how the other party performs; instead, it says, "This is what I've chosen to do. I'm going to do this no matter what. This is what I do because it is something that I promised I would do. End of story."

We really can live happily ever after, but we must be willing to go through the difficult times and *choose* to do what it takes to come out on the other side happily ever after.

GROUP DISCUSSION

1. Briefly share your thoughts and response to what you learned in the video regarding the primary difference between commitment and covenant.

2. Why is it important to go into marriage with the attitude of "this is going to work"? How does having an "escape clause" weaken marriage?

3. Explain how commitment is a feeling AND also a decision.

4. According to Willie and Elaine, constraints are boundaries that give stability – that keep us in our relationship – and that maintain the strength and integrity of our marriage. Share examples of constraints.

5. Staying together because of the kids is a constraint. In what ways does staying together benefit the kids? And what should a husband and wife be doing with their relationship after having chosen to stay together?

6. What role do constraints play when our dedication to our spouse is low?

7. Marriage is like the stock market – we don't panic and quit when things get tough. Discuss what investing in marriage for the long haul looks like.

8. What do you think of the idea that marriage is a relationship between two imperfect people who inevitably will say or do something that hurts the other person?

9. In the video, Mike said: "My spouse would never intentionally hurt me, so I'm going to give him/her the benefit of the doubt." How does this response reinforce commitment?

10. Explain how constraint, by keeping us in our marriage, can lead to feelings of being stuck or trapped in an unhappy relationship. What can we do to prevent that from happening?

11. Explain the difference between "sticking" and feeling "stuck."

12. What are some ways we can "start right" to make our relationships better and make the marriage "stick?"

ASSIGNMENT ONE: CONNECTING WITH YOURSELF

Self-Reflection Questions

According to the research, people who choose to stay together, and work to improve their marriage, do better; their kids do better; they earn and save more money; they are happier; and they have better sex.

Healthy and long-lasting marriages create stable homes, communities, and churches. Additionally, according to the research, children who grow up with both parents do better in school, make better choices, and have better life chances and opportunities.

1. With everything you've heard and learned during this series, would you say your commitment to your marriage is more like a business contract or a sacred covenant?

2. Is divorce an option for you?

3. What is your personal response to the idea that marriage is a relationship between two imperfect people? How will this affect your relationship with your spouse moving forward into the future?

4. Are you committed to investing in your marriage for the long haul?

5. What should you do if you feel stuck or trapped in an unhappy marriage?

6. After all of these weeks in this Mad About Marriage small group, write two or three sentences about what marriage means to you, along with some hopes and dreams you have for your own marriage.

ASSIGNMENT TWO:
PART I: CONNECTING WITH YOUR SPOUSE

For the first part of this assignment, go somewhere you both really enjoy. Find an environment that makes you feel happy and warms your hearts. Then discuss your personal self-reflection questions with each other.

1. Casually share your thoughts about your marriage and what you have learned these past few weeks about relationships in general. Also, share any special insights you've gained about your own relationship.

2. What are two or three things you can do to continue strengthening your marriage so you can live happily ever after?

3. Acknowledge that you are two imperfect people who will make mistakes from time to time, but who are also committed to building an amazing life together.

4. Adopt this code to have a healthy marriage:

    § "I will never intentionally hurt my spouse."

    § "I know that my spouse would never intentionally hurt me, so I'm always going to give him/her the benefit of the doubt."

5. Reaffirm your commitment to each other. Decide that your marital past does not equal your marital future. Give each other the gift of a fresh start; a new beginning built upon a foundation of unconditional love and the sacred promise you made to each other. Consider renewing your commitment to each other in this special moment.

ASSIGNMENT TWO:
PART II: CONNECTING WITH YOUR SPOUSE

This assignment is fun and easy. Go do something fun together right now! Go for a walk or a drive, get some ice cream – just go have some fun! And while you're having fun, schedule a date with each other for next week, and do your best to make it a weekly habit.

CATALYST

Based on what we've learned in session six, here are some reminders, questions, or action steps to get you from where you are to where you want to be, from having a good marriage to having a great marriage. Choose one or two to focus on this week.

1. Remember, marriage is a relationship between two imperfect people.
2. Remember, divorce is not an option.
3. Remember to invest in the long haul.
4. Remember, constraints are healthy IF you work on improving your marriage during the low times.
5. Remember, happily ever after is possible, but it takes commitment.
6. Remember to have fun with your spouse.
7. Remember to plan a weekly date with your spouse.
8. Remember to give your spouse the benefit of the doubt by following this code:
    - § "I will never intentionally hurt my spouse."
    - § I know my spouse would never intentionally hurt me, so I'll always give him/her the benefit of the doubt."
9. Remember to love your spouse unconditionally.
10. Remember, your marital past does not equal your marital future.
11. Remember to forgive yourself and your spouse often.
12. Remember to give your marriage a fresh start daily.
13. Remember to love, honor, and respect one another.
14. Remember: You can be madly in love for the rest of your life!

Resources

§ *Marriage In God's Hands*, Willie and Elaine Oliver

§ www.AdventistFamilyMinistries.org

Flip the Switch – Conclusion

At the beginning of this book we asked a question: "What is your attitude toward your marriage today?" Now, as we conclude the book, we are asking the same question: "What is your attitude toward your marriage?" Has it changed?

We hope the exercises and advice found in this guidebook have been helpful, and it is our prayer that the series has started you on a path to making your marriage everything you dreamed it could be.

Remember, your marriage will be exactly what you make it. You are in charge of your attitude, and you are in charge of exactly how good or how bad your marriage is to become. It's up to you!

It's true – you really can choose to flip the switch from "just plain mad" to "madly in love forever." It may take some hard work, but believe us when we say it is worth every bit of effort you expend.

So, don't let this be the end of your marriage work. Decide every day to choose the right attitude and to do the right things to make your marriage everything it was created to be. With God's help and by His grace, you can do it!

Mike and Gayle

ALSO AVAILABLE

Mantras for Marriage: Mike and Gayle Tucker's newest book shares the "Mantras" or "slogans" that have become the guiding principle of successful marriages. Learn how to create a mantra that fits who you are as a couple and where you wish your relationship to be.

Mad About Marriage: Adapted from their successful Mad About Marriage weekend seminars, Mike and Gayle Tucker's book on Marriage helps couples take their marriage from "just plain mad" to "madly in love." They address some of the issues that are wreaking havoc in American homes today. You will find yourself recommitted and more in love with your spouse.

FREE ONLINE RESOURCES

MadAboutMarriage.com

Weekly Tips and Blog: Enrich your marriage with weekly tips designed to flip the switch from "just plain mad" to "madly in love" forever!

Free E-mail Publications: Sign up for newsletters on marriage and the relevant topics of the day. Keep informed about Mad About Marriage seminar locations and the *Mad About Marriage* television series.

Mad About Marriage Episodes: *Lifestyle Magazine: Mad About Marriage* television episodes are aired weekly/daily on TBN, Hope Channel and various networks nationwide. Stream the show archives on the website or from the *Lifestyle Magazine* Roku channel.

Faith For Today Products: Find new resources for interpersonal relationships, family, health and spiritual well-being through other books and products available from Faith For Today.

MadAboutMarriage.com | FaithForToday.tv

SHARE YOUR THOUGHTS

With the Authors: Your comments will be forwarded to the author when you send them to:
info@MadAboutMarriage.com

With Faith For Today: Submit comments or requests to:
info@FaithForToday.tv

NOTES

NOTES